www.finishinglinepress.com

CROW MIND

poems by

Tobey Hiller

Finishing Line Press
Georgetown, Kentucky

CROW MIND

ACKNOWLEDGMENTS

"Mr. Crow Wipes His Beak," "I Read, He Plays," "I Wonder," and "Last Year's
Sorrow" in *Canary* (Winter Issue, 2015)
"The Habits of Crows" in *Askew* (2016)
"Luster," "Crawdaddy Crow," and "The Sun Burglar, the Brothers of
Sleeplessness, Hook Houdini" in *naturewriting.com* (5.25.18)
"Luster" also appears in *The Marin Poetry Center Anthology* (2019)

Publisher: Leah Maines
Editor: Christen Kincaid
Cover Art: Jeffrey Long
Author Photo: Phillip B. Ziegler
Cover Design: Elizabeth Maines McCleavy

Printed in the USA on acid-free paper.
Order online: www.finishinglinepress.com
        also available on amazon.com

Author inquiries and mail orders:
Finishing Line Press
P. O. Box 1626
Georgetown, Kentucky 40324
U. S. A.

Table of Contents

*These poems are dedicated to the memory of the poet
Donald Schenker (1930-1993).*

Mind Floats Up

Mind floats up, above the eggs & toast.
Bees work the lavender.
Crow calls.
Thought flits, testy, then
            gathers, fourfoots down to
something I've forgotten now.
Wind feathers sunbright leaves.
Crow and me (as Don would say),
we start the day.

Mr. Crow Wipes His Beak

Mr. Crow wipes his trusty beak, this side, that,
on the fence, struts
with his rolling gait
down the fence-top highway,
bull-necked Sweeney among no nightingales,
looking here, there.

Surveying his territory?
Hawk-checking?
Alert to the shadowed flicker
I must make on the window
when carefully carefully
all slow molasses
I move to keep him in sight?

What
flits in his black and burnished
mind? What shines
in his sight?

Sharp

of beak & plumage,
wing points prod air,
tripartite claws
swing a dinosaur
swagger.

Blues Brothers
shoulders, wit
as wide as wild.
Crow's all point & luster.
This is not tuxedo
or mourning garb,
nor a dancer's thin whiplash
darkness.
More black cat ink
and strut.
He knows who goes there.
What's what.

His Dark Mistress

She's sleek as tempered steel,
black as any midnight thought, empress
of the South or Ninja, gleams
deep shine, a dark more definite
than light's absence. Shoulders
not so broad as his, defers it seems
to his rough speech. But I
imagine her alternate path
through day's branched gold
and green of observation,
arrow of her own.

Her unique call
he learns
and yearns for
when uncalled-for silence erupts
in Caw-dor Castle.
With it, he names her, calls her;
where-s't, wide-call, call!

At the water, she takes second sips.
He bounces over her, short umbrella hop.
Waits, watches surrounding air, trees, any
flick-shadow of interlope arrival,
as she drinks.

When a crow the flock knows dies,
they gather.
They make noise. Caco-
phony.

One, in captivity,
fell silent four days
when his mate died.

Luster

Crow shines as the darkest star.
Light burrows into the coal of him,
blacks down to diamond,
bounces off
his sharp facets
into midnight's noon.
It is his cloak and dagger.
He wears it on his shoulders
the way Mercury wore flight & cunning:
armor, trumpet, name
of what black is
underneath the sun.

Luster's reason
is without preamble—
the first cause is always light.

His Philosophy

Yesterday I lost a poem about Crow—
the second one I wrote. Gone for good.
Losing, finding, management & mis-, order, chaos, regret,
revenge and unsubstantiation of materia, evanescence . . .
memory's many treacheries, not to mention
language: well, we'll stay away from Wittgenstein,
whom I am not competent to parse.

Hume's more like it when it comes to Crow:
sensation, idea, a clear line tween
what comes to beak and what arrives in head.

This poem I lost:
sometimes it's backs of envelopes, scraps of post-it, bits of paper,
    scribbles
on the moment's walls. Chitbits
stuck in paper haystacks and desk tide scruffle.
Easy to lose track. Let them lie. Go away. Forget.
Or poke them, half-plucked, into unfiled piles,
neglected as an unfinished outbuilding
blurring under rain.

Visitors come. They go. Dinner gets cooked. Newspapers
fold their old news into the trash.

Scraps go up in every smoke the day exhales.
Combustion and evaporation's
the way of things. Crow knows this
when he looks at water
shrunk to slime.

It was such a good one.
Of course.

Crow, if he misses that delectable mouse, bounces up and caws.
A loud complaint: challenge to the morning's misrule? call to mates
to sympathize? But then, like all natural athletes and realists,
like Hume or summer or politicians, he moves on.

Regrets fill no bellies.
Blue sky calls.

Their Drinking

Drinking,
they stretch inkblack slink throats back,
tip beaks high to sky,
like any bantam
any songbird
any egret turkey pheasant jay,
as all their broad nation does.

Except the hummingbird,
whose acrobatic helicopter sip
with that anteater tongue
is a legend
in all backyards
and spider sagas.

Crow doesn't tell
that story. It's
his own he knows
by heart.

Worry

Mr. Crow and his gal fly in,
loaded with bread bits to wash.
Maybe it's Hansel & Gretel's,
I don't know.

I want to tell them—wherever
they're getting that bread—it's not
good for them. I've always
had two cents to donate
to the conversation. But oh well,
I can only say ciao in crow.
It's a loud greeting, and the next
part of the alphabet involves a hop
higher than any wingless creature can go.

The Habits of Crows

I just found part of a mouse,
tail (ringed in perfect circles
descending in size to the minute)
and feet, long toes pointed uselessly,
still attached to a picked-away sheath
of skin, floating in the water basin
Mr. & Mrs. Crow use to wash their food.

Usually it's bread, or wild onion stalks.
But Crow's omnivorous, and inventive.
He uses tools. He washes his food. He lives
everywhere. His flock increases. He's smart.
Like us.
A murder of crows, we call it.

Crow Sees Blue

It took us eons
to name blue. Homer
called them "wine-dark seas"- dark
red. Or crimson deep.
Birds see more spectra than we do.
They have more cones. As painters,
they would be wilder than Monet.
So Crow, what he loves, what she sees—
must be shelter of many fluttered greens
tranced wing-nesting flights of blue
black and silver and mouse-gray beyond
our dusk and shadows
with sharpest azure & all its
brother sister colors
belonging to
and
yes, possessing
him,
too.

I Read, He Plays

While Crow—or some relative—
slides down windshields and roofs and hills in the snow,
or bites some unsuspecting dog's tail in the park,
or chases cats around a courtyard
and waddles off all a-cackle,
I watch him online,
researching the habits of his kind.

The way he figures me out
is just what I did when I was small:
he watches.
Crows look.
Notice pattern.
Think: today *is*; tomorrow
will be. And then
Crow tests it.

I know this because Crow's out there,
watching me watching.
When I was young,
I slid down snowbanks too.
Slippery's its own reward.

Crow knows we're dangerous.
And not, sometimes.
He recognizes faces, counts
enemy & friend. If Crow
were larger than me,
I'd watch him like that too.

Mr. Crow Imitates a Cat I Had

I'm out watering plants.
He ambles along the fence,
angles sidewise glint of eye and expectation.

So? *his glance says* So?
(I speak that much crow.)
He enlarges.
Priorities slipped your mind?
Can you count to six?
Breakfast is number one.
My morning necessities, please.
Now would be the time
to fill that water basin.
I know you can use that snakey
toolwater thing
to more purpose.
Hop to.

Crow's World

I do not mention him today.
About that, says Mr. Crow,
who cares?

The Difference between Us

Though there's an historic drought in California,
where we live, Crow and I,
I was unable to resist the little pepper plant,
the Japanese eggplant (so elegant, edible & comic all at once—
those purple Groucho noses), a squash plant that will splash
everywhere, & just a few others, not to mention all the flowers nodding
gorgeous heads I've already planted in my garden, though no one had
    the milkweed
I'd set out to buy to feed the Monarch butterflies, who can barely find
their archipelago of food now in the orange muscle of their migration
    south
along the de-weeded, insect-toxic corn fields.

Crow notices the wild onion has been mowed down; he switches
to mice, spiders, purloined bread, the odd blown-by-night hamburger
    wrapper.

I'll water sparingly. I save run-off from the shower.
Resource. Survival. Think outside the box.
Greed. For dinner. For color. For bounce and flurry,
the everness of spring. We both
do what we want, but I,
with my hope and so-called moral sense,
do it anyway.

Crawdaddy Crow

sidles sidewise downfence,
watching Squirrel pump his loud tail.
Nuts are the subject
and object, noise (chit chit & caw) the notice
of what will out.
Crawdaddy keeps his cool,
flaunts his black black epaulets,
lets wind carry its feather news
his way. The strategy's
the double deal
behind bark's
blank.

When Crow was knighted
he did not bow.
He noticed that the sword,
descending, truncated
Grandfather tree.
He's good at
side effects.
He kept his eye on where
the nuts fell, watched the telltale flag
of Squirrel's tail.

When he croaked "nevermore"
this was taken at face value,
though Sir Crawdaddy Crow knows
nothing happens in heaven
or earth
that will happen never more.

Crow and Naught

Crow can count to six.
Or so they say.
I have not seen it.

Once a day I fill the basin.
The sun comes up. The sun goes down.
It hangs alive in sky.
That's three.
Once yesterday a hawk flew over.
Four caws. Then more than six.
Five crows mobbed him.
Yesterday no poem.
No bread
in the water.
As for zero, it's something
crow understands only
with his belly. I
with my pen.

She Bathes

They both fly in, drink, flex, peck, jump
up on the rock, jockey. She el-
bows him a bit, keeps
jumping down into water,
& after the usual while
he flies off.
She stays.
Gingerly, she steps in-
to the small waters.

Stands ankle-deep,
sits, fluffs
her feathers. Steps
out, steps in,
glances here, glitters there.
      Plumply, she
settles down, flings water-drops off wing-tip,
shimmies, turns.
                To me
she seems languorous
taking it long and
slow, eros in
an interval away
from all clutter
of nest, food, caw, him.

Meticulous beak trims & tidies—she preens
wing feathers, plucks and presses—
you might say primp, you might say
pleasure, you might
say
self.

He flies back and forth transversely
a few times,
calls.
Other crows watch from
branches. Maybe
they're guarding, may-
be they follow tribal rules.

But she's alone,
here
in her bath
in her own crow mind,
and what
she thinks—
whether flight
or nest
or itch—
is hers alone.

I Wonder

Squirrel no longer runs along our fence
to the water. Squirrel lost a recent altercation
with Mr. Midnight and his uncoy mistress.
The little birds, even the plump enthusiastic robins,
opt for any early worm, but
do not bathe these days
at Crow's watering hole.

Does he change the world,
cause bird migrations, leave new
cities spread wide and pecked,
devastated kingdoms?

His shoulders glint.
He struts and steals and figures things out.
Familiarity breeds doubt.

How Crow Became Legion

's a saga of many stanzas, with long slogs
between boughs of the slow millennia, and sky
to tell it to. His tribe likes congregation, finds ways
to gather plainwise and catch as catch canny, sweeps a wide soar
from veldt to forest, down to meadow and up to sky, gypsy
bursts of clatterblack, minor thieveries, and rumors of war till the
    river's owned. Behind
the garbage dump will do just fine, string and bottle's just two of what
is underfoot. Four and twenty will burst
out of any pie. He calls it Saga of the Noonday Raven:
blackest epic of them all.

His eye's worldwide.
His heart's as red and pulsing
with all the heart's four and twenty chariots of desire
as yours and mine.

Come brother, come sister
he says, I will show you how
to grow
and grow.

Crow's Speech

Sometimes Crow imitates starlings, or dogs.
Ruff, ruff.
Or us: cacrow? he says. 'Lo?
Crow's rasp, crow's insistence,
his bugle call, his rap and chant and chorus
his thud and joke and unapologetic blast
and bleat—
if that loud panoply
were the only bird calls
we heard,
would we call it song?
Well, it is, says Crow.
I'm a bird.

Absence

I went away. I
made arrangements for the plants
and for the corvid waters.
I came back.

Three days. Four.
I have not seen them.
This could be happenstance, though I've been
vigilant. No, I don't sit waiting
by the window. But
my mind's flight slips
over some crow horizon
where absence breaks a vow.

Where are they?
Have they deserted me?
Or was I the one whose journey
broke an ancient unlorn promise?

Did the watering fail?
Did other destinations deploy their promise?
Crows adapt; it's a delectation
of distance and dystopia we understand.
All this is knowledge our tribes share.

I listen for their rasp and gargle,
that clearing of the barking, graveled throat.
My name's not called above
the small and daily waters.

There!

they are! Just as, in
my waiting, I rewrite
the plaint & plea of absence.
2 crows . . . but

is it Crow? Could it be
some young ones? Teenagers starting everything
out fresh? Kith and kin
but not Crow and Mrs. whom I know? Who

will speak my name
when I am gone?

Are You?

Crow, I do not know.
Are you as I see you?
How do you see me?

Eyes glance, nerves flutter, and we fly
toward something shared. The blue,
the hunger, is it wonder? Curiosity's
nerve? Our backyard in common? Together
in the feather with your lady, and she with that
dark and caw of flight, that swoop to where
I set out water, that waiting I do to see
what's next in crow agenda, that is
me and you.
What is together
in this world of watch and hope
and slim chance
of water's sweet
and blue's clasp
of comfort?

Do we both think together,
some wonder of what?
Together is the only
ownership, I think.

You fly off (not high, but jump
into swoop, stoop low)
to sky.

I stand. I
wonder.
Not why. How
and can we
know, Crow?
though all's fine

simply
with the come
and go.

Last Year's Sorrow

Was it theirs?
Last year I found a crow baby,
desiccate, half-buried in grass, hard by
the back garden gate. Head
thrown impossibly back, wings
hardly pinioned. Was it theirs?

Crows mate for life, and
crowbabies grow up slow. For three or four
years they teenage between zoom and
fortune, play fake doom
and boom
before they settle down
to all that family labor.
This year, did they
send their babies successful into sky?

An ancestor of mine, Zilpah Hall,
married at 24 in 1804,
bore 9 children,
Ardelia, Lydia, Alonzo,
Ruth, Abigail, Sarah,
Rowena, Mary, Fanny.
She was always
pregnant, bearing, suckling.
Alonzo, the boy,
died at just over 1 year.
I know this (though not
how Zilpah wept,
binding up her sorrow
in silence, bent
over the washtub,
tears
dripping into laundry)
because his sister Rowena
made a sampler
listing her family's names,
and their dates.

At the bottom
is a prayer for Alonzo.

This is my prayer
for the crow baby,
dead before he fledged,
and for his siblings,
who fly now,
and argue,
and bathe,
and watch me,
for the hope
I bring as water.

The Sun Burglar, the Brothers of Sleeplessness, Hook Houdini

Crow has always known how to tell a story.
How to burgle Sky Chief, become his daughter's
fussy child, fly like a plucked black hair
through the smoke hole
and seed the unlit sky with stars and moon.
How to tell Odin what to think (Hugin)
& what to remember (Munin)
after the pair
circle the whole world while the
Hammer-Thrower sleeps.

First Nations know he can carve a canoe
that will grow a foot to walk right out
of drowning waters, survive
the scheming uncle, talk dirty
to Prudella's kicking foot,
and, clothed in his cloak of trickeries
all the way through any history's epic,
transform your car
into a nutcracker.

Researchers watch Crow solve it:
use rocks to weight a board till it slants
to drop the needed stick, displace
water in a beaker with one stone, two, three
till what he wants floats within reach,
bend a hook and using it with string,
lift food out of a tube. Or
in the wild,
dig a morsel out of a tree
with a forked stick, poke it out
of an anthill,
or pretend to stash it while
another bird watches, because thievery's
eye comes easily to him.

Shaman, trickster, quick study,
Mr. Blackeyed Sleek of Smarts
still transforms the world
we like to call our own.

Dear Ted,

this is not your story.
Not
your song.
His skull is large.
His kingdom (where black & bright exist
all mixed)
full.
We are wild, yes,
and the black—so black
it's easy to dig out only guts & blood,
all the hope deposed by death —
includes the
bright unceasing blue.
Nothing's one way
or the other.
Oh well,
crow glances up
at sky,
which covers all of us,
and flies.

Crow knows

what?
He shows
a black box fox-
like glance to me,
dives into
sky, the large
goodbye of caw
and go. The world's
a place
of high and low,
and all that's
in between my here,
his there:
well, it's
a cascade made
of starstuff legacies
invisible to proof
whose mineral and liquid names
I do not know.
Let's call it
this morning's sweet swing low
the blind man's touch and go
that other skyhigh thing we know—
all of us
under great god sun
featherflanked by mother rain
named playful when we can
by the glide and glad
of snow.

Crow

never says goodbye.
Just flies off.
Jumps off the fence down into air like heavy aircraft taking off, drops
out of sight,
lifts,
rows up into sky and disappears
into his
green, his
air of planks & hills, his
under sun everyday, his
memory
of me,
and all.

Crow Mind is a backyard conversation between crow and poet, full of delight, curiosity, play, sorrow and meditation on our species' shared habits, both charming and ruthless—a lovesong to the wild world we find right up against our doorsteps. Tobey Hiller's poems are wide-ranging: humorous, philosophical, probing. She sees human beings as part of a natural and animal community full of both dire challenge and constant beauty, and she has an abiding interest in our emotional and cognitive relationship to the creatures and places around us. These poems tell us how meeting, observing, sharing with the others who share our world are both deeply satisfying experiences and essential to the well-being of our planet.

She is the author of three books of poetry, *Crossings* (Oyez), *Certain Weathers* (Oyez) and *Aqueduct* (Clear Mt. Press, with drawings by Joanna Axtmann) and a novel, *Charlie's Exit* (EdgeWork, Boulder). About her work, the late David Meltzer said "a clear impassioned intent underlies the work as a whole . . . the lyric of accomplished grace and concern, they insist their music against the ongoing emptying-out of language our era contends with daily."

Her work has appeared in the anthologies:
Resurgent: New Writing by Women (University of Illinois Press); *Through the Mill* (The Mill Press); *Left Hand Maps: San Francisco Bay Area Poets* (A Small Garlic Press); *Literature and its Writers* (Bedford Books); and most recently, *Fire and Rain: Ecopoetry of California* (Scarlet Tanager Books, 2018) and *The Wild*, (Marin Poetry Center, 2019).

Her poetry has appeared in numerous magazines and journals, print and online. Her poems won early honors from *S.F. Poetry* and *Embers Magazine*, and three of her stories have been short-listed for prizes.

Her non-fiction writing includes an *Afterword* for the Signet Classic

Edition of Jack London's stories, various reviews and writings on fiction and psychology, and a book on couples therapy, with Phillip Ziegler, *Recreating Partnership, A Collaborative Approach to Couples Therapy* (W.W. Norton).

Born on the East Coast, she migrated west and has lived for years in northern California. She worked for many years as a psychodramatist, group leader and therapist, and she and her husband have two children and four grandchildren.